D0127923

Self-Esteem:
The Power to Be Your Best

NATIONAL PRESS PUBLICATIONS
A Division of Rockhurst College Continuing Education Center, Inc.
6901 West 63rd Street • P.O. Box 2949 • Shawnee Mission, Kansas 66201-1349
1-800-258-7248 • 1-913-432-7757

National Press Publications endorses non-sexist language. In an effort to make this handbook clear, consistent and easy to read, we've used "he" throughout the odd-numbered chapters and "she" throughout the even-numbered chapters. The copy is not intended to be sexist.

Self-Esteem: *The Power to Be Your Best*
Published by National Press Publications, Inc.
Copyright 1995 National Press Publications, Inc.
A Division of Rockhurst College Continuing Education Center, Inc.

Printed in the United States of America

28 27 26 25 24 23

ISBN 1-55852-152-6

TABLE OF CONTENTS

INTRODUCTION

When you look in the mirror, what do you see? Someone short or tall, thin or lumpy, dark- or fair-skinned, blonde or brunette, somewhere in between perhaps? These physical characteristics make up your outer self — what's visible to the world.

Now look a little deeper — into your eyes, your heart, your soul. What do you see there? Are you serious or fun-loving, passive or aggressive, volatile or even-tempered? These personality traits or emotional tendencies make up your inner self — what you project to the world.

Whatever your physical or emotional characteristics are, you need to like and accept what you see in the mirror. In other words, you need a healthy dose of self-esteem. Unfortunately, the majority of us lack the required daily dosage. That's why this book was written. Think of it as a prescription for acquiring the self-esteem necessary to have a truly happy and productive life, both for yourself and for those around you.

The vision you currently have of yourself probably springs from your childhood and the guilt, fear, criticism and resentment most children experience. To begin building up your self-esteem, you must honestly confront your feelings and emotions. Although it's a time-consuming process, think of it as an investment in the future. The self-esteem you'll gain is something well worth passing onto your children.

Through its proven techniques and probing exercises, this book shows you how to bolster your self-esteem and enhance your self-image. It also explains how goal-setting helps you focus on those things about yourself that you want to improve. As the old song goes, "Accentuate the positive, eliminate the negative."

With poor self-esteem, you are your own worst enemy. A healthy sense of self allows you to become your own best friend — someone you and others trust, respect and admire.

After reading this chapter, you will learn:

☑ the definition of self-esteem

☑ the symptoms of low self-esteem

☑ possible past causes of low self-esteem

1 WHAT IS SELF-ESTEEM AND WHY IS IT ESSENTIAL?

How many times has the following scenario happened to you? You are faced with a challenge — winning a marathon, taking first place in a writing competition, getting a promotion. And then, you win, you get promoted! Often, what happens next? You tell yourself, *"I won, but I don't feel like a winner."* No matter how often you succeed, your accomplishments can't touch that person inside. And that's where it counts because that's where you really live after all the fanfare dies down.

If you look closely, you'll see the little child you were so many years ago. That little child may have some qualities that blossomed as you matured: wisdom, humor, strength of purpose, the ability to communicate well with others. No doubt that child is also like most other children … at times fearful, unsure, dependent on adults to know what to do and unaware of his own special qualities.

We'll work more with your own inner child later on, but for now you should know that within that early vision of yourself lies the seed of your self-esteem. Self-esteem is not something you can graft onto the tree of a full-fledged adult personality. You must go back and find a young branch of your impressionable childhood from which self-esteem can sprout and flourish.

What Is Self-Esteem?

Self-esteem means truly loving and valuing yourself. This is quite different from being an obnoxious, overblown egomaniac. Self-esteem means you have accepted yourself as you are but continue to work on improving yourself. While that process is taking place, you have a healthy appreciation for yourself — your best qualities and your finest achievements.

To determine if your self-esteem is healthy and in good working order, consider the following:

1. **Do you accept yourself for what you are?**

   This includes your looks and feelings, your strengths and weaknesses.

2. **Do you accept credit for what you do?**

   When people ask, "What do you do?" do you sound apologetic or unworthy?

3. **Do you take time out to recognize your hard work?**

   Or do you still feel you don't quite measure up? If you live only to meet others' expectations, you'll never meet your own.

4. **Can you turn setbacks into victories?**

   Successful people see problems as opportunities. Look at what you learned from your latest setback. Perhaps you now know how to better manage your coworkers; perhaps you understand a technical function of your job you never knew before.

Self-Esteem Means a Healthy Self-Image

Our self-image doesn't come from the mirror. It comes from within. Lack of self-esteem is like looking into a "trick" mirror at a carnival fun house. No matter how thin you are, you look in the mirror and see the same overweight/unacceptable person.

Take a minute to profile your self-image. Circle the number that reflects how you routinely act.

1. I constantly fantasize about what my life will be like after I've lost 20 pounds, met the right person or bought a new car.

1	2	3	4	5
Never				Often

2. I continually refine my work so that everyone will think it's perfect.

1	2	3	4	5
Never				Often

3. I take risks.

1	2	3	4	5
Often				Never

4. I'm aware that I walk with slumped shoulders, use limited eye contact and experience physical discomfort.

1	2	3	4	5
Never				Often

TOTAL _____

Reflections

The higher scores indicate behaviors that stand in the way of reaching and maintaining a healthy self-esteem. Learn to make the most of your immediate situation by learning to value yourself as you are at this moment. Avoid perfectionism. Instead, strive to improve. As part of this process, become aware of your nonverbal communications, for example, the way you stand or the level of energy you project.

Excessive concerns about aspects of your personal and professional life that result in perfectionism — being intolerant of one's own and others' mistakes — can mean your self-image is dependent on others' opinions of you, rather than being grounded within.

When Your Worst Enemy Is You

If you think your self-image could use some improvement, realize you're not alone. We're constantly bombarded by messages from the media, as well as from real life, telling us it's easy to be richer, thinner, younger, more successful, more sexually attractive, more socially accepted, etc. As a result, some of us are convinced that others will find us fascinating if we use expensive moisturizers, drive certain cars, wear the right clothes or perfume or work out at celebrity-packed health clubs.

When our criticism turns inward for whatever reason, we pronounce harsh judgments on ourselves and engage in self-defeating, often self-fulfilling behaviors. If we're lucky, our friends may offer us some perspective with the following advice:

- *"You know, you're your own worst enemy."*

- *"You're harder on yourself than you are on others."*

- *"You expect too much from yourself. Learn to take one day at a time."*

If everyone's telling you to give yourself a break, do it! For two or three days, ignore that inner voice that says you're a bad housekeeper, an indifferent parent, an uncaring spouse. Don't be surprised if you feel guilty, scared or sad. Changing your behavior can feel threatening, especially at first.

Choose a color. Close your eyes and try to picture it. Now, <u>be</u> that color. Imagine you have become the color you chose. Write down all the qualities you ascribe to that color. Note what you do, what you are, how you make people feel. Be as forceful, passionate, intuitive or brilliant as you want to be.

Color	Qualities of Color	What I do; how I make people feel	Comments, e.g., trends, changes

Now look at what you've written. How does that color mirror certain things about you? Try doing this exercise daily. Do your color choices change? How do your emotions change? Write down your responses **in a notebook or journal** to record your feelings.

Reflections

The Price of Workaholism and Perfectionism

Workaholism and perfectionism are other symptoms of low self-esteem. Both are condoned in a workplace that values long, hard hours over personal happiness.

The devastating effects of workaholism on our family lives can no longer be ignored. When allowed to flourish, workaholism can lead to drug and alcohol abuse, emotional codependency, poor physical health, divorce and physical abuse.

To find out if you're working too long and too hard, ask yourself the following questions and record your answer on the blank line:

1. How many hours a week do I spend at my job? _____

   Whether you're a vice president or an administrative assistant, some people choose to work 10 hour days as well as on weekends. Out of middle managers, 21 percent spend between 41 and 49 hours per week at their jobs; and 53 percent spend 50 to 59 hours.

2. Do I choose to work these hours or does my company expect me to? _____ (my choice) or _____ (company's choice)

   Most workaholics begin by being externally driven, but Fortune 500 companies are wising up. They are beginning to understand that long hours lead to employee burnout and lessened effectiveness on the job.

3. Can you lower the number of hours you spend at work without putting your job in jeopardy? _____ (yes) or _____ (no)

   Ways you can improve performance and still leave at 5:30:

   • Limit time spent socializing.

   • If you're trapped in unproductive meetings, ask an attendee to take notes for you or record the meeting.

   • Opt for flex time, or work through lunch to make your day shorter. (Getting out of the rut of working the same hours can be energizing.)

4. Do you have a well-rounded life? _____ (yes) or _____ (no)

   How much time do you spend with your children? Ask yourself:

   • How much time do I spend helping my school-age children with homework each night? _____

Reflections

- Am I available on weeknights or on weekends for intramural sports or theater events or Girl Scout/Boy Scout meetings?_____

- Even if my time is limited, do I make an effort to spend time with my child? _____ (yes) or _____ (no)

- Do I make time to visit my child at school? _____ (yes) or _____ (no) *Some parents become "visiting resources" — discussing what they do for a living with their children's class.*

5. Do you have time for yourself? _____ (yes) or _____ (no)

   - Try taking a class in scuba diving or archaeology. Or just lie around the beach.

   - What about hobbies and recreation? Find something you like to do and weave it back into your life.

   - Do you schedule time to spend with community, church or social groups you enjoy? By participating, you reap the rewards of getting things done and increase your sense of personal effectiveness outside the office.

   - When was the last time you had lunch with an old school chum? _____ (date)

   - Make time for the people whose company you truly enjoy.

   - Do you take regular vacations? _____ (yes) or _____ (no)

     Start by taking just a little time off and see what happens at the office. They never knew you were gone, right? You had fun getting away, and now it's fun to come back to work. Everybody wins!

Record what trends you've noticed, and repeat this exercise on a routine basis.

Reflections

The Four Evil Fairies of Childhood

One reason we often think we're not good enough is due to the arsenal of guilt, criticism, fear and resentment we were armed with as children. Out of the hundreds of messages 2-year-olds hear from their parents in a single day, approximately 32 are positive — 432 are negative.

Throughout our childhood most of us looked upon our parents as the "good fairies" who were sent to protect and guide us. Yet by instilling guilt and fear and by passing on their critical, resentful patterns, our parents often unwittingly played the role of the "evil fairies" as well. These negative controls were intended to elicit correct behavior; instead they often promoted low self-worth.

1. **Guilt**

   If we heard messages about how "bad" we were as children, we tried to "act" in ways that would earn our parents' love and acceptance. Consequently, children who experienced a great deal of guilt were brought up to please others and to deny their own needs.

   Ask yourself how you feel when you do something simply to please yourself. Some health studies suggest that children who were brought up with a lot of guilt messages often experience sore throats, tonsillitis and thyroid problems. Our larynx is where our voice originates — the instrument by which we proclaim to others who we are.

2. **Fear**

   Children naturally want to explore, experience, ask questions and probe the world around them. Therefore, a family environment filled with fear is possibly the most damaging. As adults, our fears may translate into physical ailments such as ulcers or back problems.

Fearful adults often disguise their emotions by exaggerated bullying behavior. When confronted with a child's emotion that triggers their own fearful response, they belittle the child, calling him names rather than offering support and understanding. Fear can squelch an individual's creativity and willingness to love. You overcome fear by learning to love and value yourself.

3. Criticism

We have all been criticized by our parents and know that nothing produces such an overwhelming sense of unworthiness. Remarks like "you never do anything right" cause our self-confidence to plummet.

When under stress, we sometimes hear the same words coming out of our own mouths directed at our own children. How can we stop the flow of critical abuse that filters down from one generation to the next? Release the habit of criticism, and your self-esteem will begin to spring back to life.

4. Resentment

When we're resentful of others' success, happiness or material wealth, it means we have lost sight of our own goals and aspirations. We all possess different gifts, abilities and innate talents. Resenting others' good fortune is a barrier to our own growth and change.

When we find that resentment clouds our relationships, we need to let go of the past and all the injustices it contains. Begin affirming your own uniqueness with statements like, *"I am my own person and claim my unique place in the universe."*

So What's the Answer?

In the next few chapters, we'll examine what poor self-esteem and a negative self-image can do. We will then learn how to replace destructive behaviors with patterns of success, happiness and a healthy self-esteem.

We'll also talk about defining and achieving goals and their importance in your life. Finally, we will explore how to build self-esteem in others.

Summary

Self-esteem is linked to a healthy self-image that reflects a strong, vibrant, energized person. People with low self-esteem often have a negative self-image that can cause:

- Failure to seize upon today's opportunities by constantly fantasizing about doing things "tomorrow."

- Pefectionism — an obsession with appearance or a need to constantly do things "right."

- Communication of a negative self-image through poor body language.

Self-esteem is an important ingredient in improving not only your life, but the lives of everyone you come into contact with.

Being critical and judgmental of others is a sign of poor self-esteem. Being overly demanding of ourselves, through perfectionism or workaholism, are both classic low self-esteem syndromes.

The key to our poor opinions of ourselves can often be found in the past. How our parents treated us when we were infants and children sets the pattern for the types of relationships we may develop as adults.

If not resolved or overcome, early negative patterns established between ourselves and our parents can continue to be mirrored in the relationships we form once we're adults.

After reading this chapter, you will learn:

☑   to use visualization to increase your self-esteem

☑   to use affirmations to start making needed changes

☑   to explain why affirmations work

2 MAKING A CHANGE FOR THE BETTER

We've all heard about the power of positive thinking. Maybe you even tried "looking on the bright side" for a while and discovered that your world didn't change as quickly as your attitude. Adjusting your attitude without working on your self-esteem is simply a quick fix that can take you only a short way down the track before a major breakdown occurs.

Attitudes, like colds, are catching. When we appear strongly motivated and positive, others want to be around us and bask in the reflected glow of our self-confidence. Similarly, when our self-esteem is low, it's easy to draw others into the vortex of our negativity.

Think of the road to success as a smooth, straight surface paved with high self-esteem. You know there will be obstacles, pitfalls and difficult patches to be negotiated, yet you have what it takes to get there — *belief in yourself and a positive attitude.*

Live the Life You Choose

If, as a child, the only time you received any attention was when you were sick or hurting, then you might subconsciously place yourself in situations as an adult in which you're perpetually victimized. However, understand and recognize that you're free to choose and free to change.

What's holding you back from making these sweeping changes for the better, from leading a more complete, fulfilling life? One answer is your subconscious mind — that industrious little genie who whispers self-defeating messages in your ear, who erodes what confidence you may have developed and, in general, helps you realize your worst fears about yourself.

So, how can the freedom to choose ever reprogram itself to counteract the dutiful genie who thinks it's working for a bad, lazy, morally reprehensible boss? The answer lies in words and pictures. Visualize and verbalize consciously, and you'll change the structure of your subconscious!

Starting Here; Starting Now

If you always thought that "someday" you would get it all together — when you were more financially secure, when you were thinner, when your children were grown — realize that the only time you have control over is this very second. Begin today to have a future filled with security, purpose, love and fulfillment.

Begin to love yourself consciously. Think of yourself as a Christopher Columbus, about to undertake an exciting new voyage of self-discovery. You'll be able to weather any stormy sea that threatens your self-esteem as long as you know a few basic laws about universal self-love.

What we think about ourselves becomes the truth.

It's not what others say about us, it's what we say about ourselves that matters. If you think you're unworthy, you'll never feel good about yourself, no matter how many outer trappings of success you acquire. Conversely, if you love yourself, others will find you lovable too.

Visualization

Our subconscious mind dutifully constructs our reality from the pictures we give it. You can use visualization to your advantage, either as a separate exercise or in conjunction with your affirmations.

As Emmett Fox, one of the pioneers of positive thinking, wrote, *"The secret of successful living is to build up the mental equivalent of what you want; and to get rid of the mental equivalent of what you do not want."*

How Visualization Works

To make visualization work for you, follow these simple guidelines:

Relax and breathe. Find some place in your house where you can be comfortable and have privacy. Create whatever kind of environment feels right for meditation and relaxation. Light a candle if you like, or burn incense. You can play soft, soothing music — whatever creates an atmosphere of peace and tranquility. Now begin regulating your breathing. As you inhale more deeply, visualize yourself going within — to the most personal, private part of you. Imagine yourself going deeper, like a deepsea diver, until you're submerged in your own essence.

Allow yourself to feel what you need. Begin to feel what it is you most deeply want or care about. Is it to be more nurturing? Is it to unleash your creative abilities? Don't worry about whether it makes "sense" or is in keeping with your present life-style. Pay attention to how "good" it feels — how fulfilled this new concept makes you feel.

Visualize in detail. Perhaps you want to write a book that will help people and be an enormous success. Don't worry about the book's details. Those problems are for your conscious mind to resolve. See your book being read by millions of people who are grateful for the information you've given them. See yourself at book signings and on talk shows, responding to the success your book has generated.

Try This Visualization Exercise

Using a photograph of yourself as an infant, close your eyes and hold the picture close to your heart. Breathe deeply, concentrating on how it must have felt to be a baby. Imagine how new, strange and exciting the world appeared to you then. Now look into this child's eyes and realize there is only one thing this baby wants from the adult you —unconditional love. Visualize holding yourself as a baby in your own arms. Tell the baby how much you love and care. Admire everything about this perfect child.

Keep the photograph where you can see it often and repeat the exercise. Record the feelings that surfaced. You may feel a "bonding" between this early part of you and the adult you now are. This helps you get in touch with the part of you who was an infant. As the child within begins to have his needs met, how does your behavior change? Record these behaviors too. Are you less critical of others?

Date	Feelings that surfaced	Changes I've noted in my current behavior
_____	_____	_____
_____	_____	_____
_____	_____	_____
_____	_____	_____
_____	_____	_____
_____	_____	_____

Reflections

Whatever your fantasy goal, make it real by making it detailed. Cut out pictures from magazines. Perhaps you're thinking about buying a log cabin in the Rockies, or perhaps you admire the movies Steven Spielberg makes. Look for pictures of cabins or film directors to "flick the switch" of your subconscious. When you find a picture that enhances your visualization, tear it out and pin it up on a bulletin board where you can see it. You might also want to keep the pictures in a special "dream album."

Make visualization a regular part of your life

The more time you spend visualizing your goal, the more real it will become. When you start spending time on a regular basis visualizing your goals, they become a familiar place where you can recharge and relax. Daily updates and detailing help keep you in the present.

Visualizing your success

At the end of the day, sit quietly in a comfortable chair. Concentrate on your breathing and gradually regulate your rate of respiration. Notice how your heartbeat slows down. Feel all the day's anxieties and cares float away from you. Now, very quietly, begin imagining the "ideal" you.

Perhaps you always intended to get into shape, but now it's practically too late. Visualize yourself jogging each day. Is this enough or does it lead to something more? Do you see yourself entering the Boston marathon or a triathlon competition? Let your imagination go. Take yourself to the pinnacle of success in everything you visualize.

Visualization can be a powerful means of physical and spiritual healing. Cancer patients are frequently taught positive self-imaging as part of their therapy in coping with this deadly disease.

One of the most important elements in getting visualizations to work for you is the ability to let go, no matter how chaotic or unsatisfying your life seems. Proclaiming this as an affirmation in the midst of a stressful situation allows you to stop worrying, to let go and allow more positive energy to flow through you.

Visualization can be expanded by identifying a goal that is important to you.

Focus on the goal mentally so that you can write it down in a simple sentence: *"Our family is enjoying the space and beauty of our new home."*

To make more of an impact on your subconscious, it helps if you can find a picture of the kind of house you want. It should be one that is affordable, yet meets your needs. When you find the ideal picture, cut it out and paste it on a piece of cardboard. Use it in your daily visualization. Cut out photos of yourself and your family and place them in and around the house. This technique is called "treasure mapping" — making the ideal "real" by using your imagination and power to visualize.

Continue by reviewing the visualization guidelines in the section "How Visualization Works."

Goal:

_____

_____

_____

Photo or visual used:

_____

Progress on reaching goal:

Date _____

Date _____

Reflections

Now sit quietly and visualize you and your family in your new home. See it in its exquisite detail — include the kinds of shrubs and flower beds you'll plant, how you'll decorate the children's rooms, the comfortable, spacious living room, the functional kitchen.

Keep your ideal scene in a notebook by your bed or hang it on the wall in the room where you meditate. Look at it often. Keep a log of any changes you make to your visualization. Record the time it takes for the visualization to become real, noting the date of your initial imaging and affirmations and the final moving day.

We create our experiences by our thoughts and feelings.

If you find yourself saying predominantly negative things, you can change this verbal pattern. Daily affirmations are an easy weapon for combating negative thinking.

Affirmations

The more you expect from situations, the more you'll achieve. Maybe you don't feel comfortable taking a strongly positive approach. You're shy, for instance, and avoid parties and gatherings where there are lots of people.

To overcome something in yourself, affirm the change. Affirmations are simple statements, usually short, declarative sentences that proclaim a fact in no uncertain terms. If, for instance, you'd like to feel more confident at social gatherings, say, *"I like people and they like me."* Repeat this sentence several times a day before the big event. Say it just before you drop off to sleep at night and when you wake up in the morning. Repeat it as you take those deep breaths before stepping into the room filled with party guests. Then watch what happens. The more you have repeated the affirmation, the more powerful its effect on your subconscious.

Here are some simple rules to follow when creating affirmations for yourself:

Affirmations must be strong and positive.

Many researchers believe affirmations that contain negatives don't work because the subconscious hears only positive statements. Consequently, if you're trying to stop smoking, don't affirm *"I am no longer craving nicotine,"* for your subconscious hears *"I am craving nicotine."* A better affirmation might be *"I am free of nicotine."*

Affirmations take place in the here and now.

By affirming a condition in the present, it becomes your reality. See how powerful this statement is, *"My job provides me with financial abundance now,"* compared to *"Next year I'll get that promotion to increase my income."*

Affirmations grow more effective with repetition.

The first time you say an affirmation it may sound strange, exotic, even slightly boastful or silly. But slowly, it becomes woven into your daily reality. Nothing is more gratifying than to reach the end of a project — taking curtain calls, autographing your new book — and realize that this moment from real life was contained in the kernel of your affirmation.

Why Affirmations Work

Affirmations work because they give your subconscious mind permission to start making long-needed changes. We need to shake up concepts that no longer work for us. Maybe you don't know exactly how you want to change, but only feel restless and dissatisfied. Try this affirmation:

"I am changing and released from my old negative beliefs."

Even if you don't realize what old beliefs you're ready to give up, merely announcing your willingness to do so opens up channels of creativity within your subconscious.

Affirmations can be said any time during the day, but they're most effective if repeated in the morning as we wake up and in the evening as we drift off to sleep.

It's a good idea to write your affirmations and keep them where you can see them often. One successful writer has covered his study with affirmations that motivate him: *"I am writing a best-selling novel;" "My work is well written and well received."*

How we view the world determines what we get.

Do you think of the world as a scary place, filled with people who are "out to get you," or do you see it as a challenging, life-enhancing environment, filled with people willing to help and even love? Whatever your definition of "what's out there," that's what you'll get!

An Example: Against his friends' advice, one professor of sociology at a Midwestern college went on a 5,000-mile solo bicycle trip in 1987 without a dime in his pocket. His mission was to prove that there is goodness and generosity in everyone, feeling that being dependent on those he met for food and shelter would help break down barriers. He asked people along the way for help and found it in the form of beds, breakfasts, grilled cheese sandwiches, hot showers and plenty of friendly chats. Among the more than 500 people he came into contact with on the road, only five refused to help.

STOP!

Don't pass these questions casually. Think hard on them. Get emotional about them!

Is there some task which you would like to do, some channel by which you would like to express yourself, but you keep holding back, feeling "I can't"?

Ask yourself, "Is this belief based upon fact — or upon an assumption or a false conclusion?"

Now ask yourself these questions:

1. Is there any reason for such a belief?

2. Am I possibly mistaken in this belief?

3. Would I come to the same conclusion about another person in a similar situation?

4. Why should I continue to act and feel as if this were true if there is no good reason to believe it?

REMEMBER:

Both behavior and feeling spring from belief. To discover the belief that is responsible for your feeling and behavior, ask yourself "Why?"

Reflections

We can make a break with the past.

No matter how deeply you've been wounded by others or what flexible decisions you've made that may have hurt others, it's important to let go of old emotions.

When we're contemplating a change, there is a tendency to negate everything we ever were. For example, you tell yourself "I *made such a stupid mistake by getting married too young"* or *"I'd never spend money as foolishly as I did two years ago."* Remember, people with high self-esteem never negate who they were or the decisions they made. The past is a powerful tool if used in the right way. It contains the answers to accepting the true you. As painful as it may be, take a long look at the changes you've been through since childhood. Embrace and accept each one.

Summary

Building your self-esteem involves more than just an attitude adjustment. Your self-esteem is regulated by your subconscious mind that, like a giant movie projector, beams your self-image back from the screen.

You can change the way you feel by changing the way you look at the world. We have control over our futures once we realize that:

- What we think about ourselves becomes the truth.

- We create our experiences by our thoughts and feelings.

- What we give out, we get back.

- We can make a break with the past.

Above all, don't reject any part of yourself or any experience from the past. Finding the true you depends on loving yourself, beginning with the innocent infant you once were. Learn to recognize and honor the child within.

Your attitude can change for the better when you fully realize that instead of being life's victim, you are living the life you choose to live. Once we realize we are free to choose, we are free to change. The only time we can make these changes is in the present. The words you choose to describe your daily life reflect the thought processes that govern each waking moment.

You can change subconscious patterning through pictures and words: by positive visualization and affirmations.

Visualization:

- Uses our imagination to provide our subconscious with new blueprints for our future through relaxation and guided imagery.

- Can become an integral part of our daily lives.

- Builds upon detail. The more sensory your visualization, the more real it is — and the more quickly it manifests itself in reality.

Affirmations:

- Should be clear and brief, strong and positive.

- Take place in the here and now.

- Are more effective with repetition.

After reading this chapter, you will learn:

 why goal-setting builds self-esteem

 how to use brainstorming to set goals effectively, and how to avoid traps

✔ how to prioritize your goals

3 GOAL-SETTING: OUR SENSE OF DIRECTION

Nothing makes your self-esteem soar more than achieving a lofty goal. Conversely, nothing can be more disheartening than failing to meet your goal.

Without clear goals, it's too easy to drift through life without making definite commitments to ourselves. As a result, we may wake up one day and find our children grown and our days pretty much our own. Yet we still haven't found the time for those golf lessons we wanted to take when we turned 30.

Why Goal-Setting Builds Self-Esteem

Perhaps the trickiest part of getting what we want out of life is deciding what it is we want. One major misconception about goal-setting is that you must know exactly what you want before you set goals. Actually, one of the best ways to clarify what you want is to set goals. While achieving them, you can constantly reevaluate whether or not your chosen path is the one you want to pursue.

Have you ever noticed that when you set a goal — a new car, a more challenging job, a vacation in Australia — it manifests more quickly? Your subconscious makes sure it's leading you straight to the perceived goal.

When it works properly, goal-setting raises your self-esteem because it:

- Challenges you to overcome patterns of failure or limitation.

- Allows you to be more tolerant of failure in other areas of your daily life.

- Gives you the confidence to set increasingly adventuresome goals, to explore areas you've neglected.

- Makes you see life as part of a process. That is, achieving a goal won't make your life perfect, but it will improve it.

- Allows you to get on with your personal development. Achieving a goal can bring new awareness of what you ultimately want.

Giving Up the Past

Remember how great it felt last spring when you finally got around to cleaning out your closets? You were amazed at the clothes you hauled out of the dark recesses. Some you had outgrown, some were hopelessly out of style, some you had been hanging on to for sentimental reasons. Then you had the garage sale and nearly all the stuff sold. The rest you trucked down to the nearest Goodwill store.

Goal-setting is a form of starting over, but it requires a kind of spring cleaning before you begin. It's called *"clearing."* For the clearing process to work on a certain belief, you must learn to do two rather dissimilar things simultaneously:

1. Accept yourself compassionately for having this belief.

2. See clearly that you're ready to let go of it because it's limiting, self-destructive and untrue.

For instance, you might have been raised by an alcoholic parent. As a child, you learned that displaying your true emotions invited an unpleasant, even violent, response. Now that you're an adult, it's still difficult for you to open up to others — particularly to partners. Most likely, as a result, you're storing a lot of anger, grief and resentment against the parent whose love you so badly needed and never received.

Take a deep breath and see if the area around your heart seems constricted. The heart represents the center of love and security for many. Therefore, when love and security are denied in some way, the loss is stored around the heart.

Or perhaps you stored your fear of criticism in your stomach. If so, you might have chronic digestive problems such as colitis, ulcers and abdominal cramps.

Repeat these affirmations, or revise them to fit your needs:

> *"I love and approve of myself. I create my own way."*
>
> *"I choose to be a winner in life."*
>
> *"I trust the process of life. I am safe."*
>
> *"I am at peace. I am calm. All is well."*

Clear out psychological blocks that are holding you back from attaining your goals. You can find out where these are by paying attention to your body. Notice where you feel the greatest amount of constriction, where tension blocks the flow of energy through your body. Take a few minutes and breathe deeply. See where you feel "tight." Is it in your chest, your arms, your head, your stomach?

Areas where I feel my body constricting	Missing love/security	Fear or criticism	Other
1.			
2.			
3.			

To get yourself moving, you must explore the area in which negative emotions are stored and reconnect the old emotions in a positive, loving way.

Continue by completing this sentence: *"The reason I can't have what I want is...."*

Breathe deeply and visualize that you're sending that breath highly charged with love, compassion and energy into the area where you feel blocked.

Next, record your negative beliefs and how you feel.

Beliefs	I feel

Example: *I'm too lazy. It's too hard.*

Beliefs	I feel
1.	1.
2.	2.
3.	3.
4.	4.

Reflections

When these feelings arise, realize they are simply "waves" of emotion and that you're floating peacefully on top of them. Breathe into them, experience them deeply, then release them. Your list may look something like this:

"I can't have what I want because..."

"I'm too lazy."

"My spouse wouldn't like it."

"It's too hard."

Look at your list again. When you feel you've finally gotten in touch with your negative beliefs, tear up the paper and throw it away or burn it. You want this part of your life to be over!

Complete this reflection by recording a couple of affirmations that replace your constricting, limiting beliefs.

Affirmation 1

_____

Affirmation 2

_____

Sit quietly in a comfortable chair with paper and pencil in your lap. At the top of the paper, write *"The reason I can't have what I want is..."* Breathe deeply and visualize that you're sending that breath highly charged with love, compassion and energy into the area where you feel blocked. Now write down the negative beliefs that come to mind. How do you feel? Don't resist feeling anger, sadness or fear.

Reflections

Forgiveness

Nothing keeps us so totally wrapped up in past problems as unexpressed feelings of anger, resentment and desire for revenge. Forgiveness is the key to letting go of the past and its power over us. Forgiveness allows us to get on with our life.

Forgiveness should be forgotten, along with the wrong that is forgiven. Forgiveness that is remembered and dwelt upon re-infects. Thus, forgiveness that is partial, or half-hearted, works no better than a partially completed surgical operation. Instead, it ought to be like a cancelled note, torn in two and burned up, so that it never can be held against one again.

Record in the space below the names of all the people who have ever harmed or mistreated you or dealt with you unjustly. Write what they did to you and why you feel resentment toward them.

Names	What he/she did	Reason(s) for resentment
1. _____	_____	_____
2. _____	_____	_____
3. _____	_____	_____
4. _____	_____	_____
5. _____	_____	_____

Now close your eyes and visualize that person clearly. Explain to him/her why you have felt hurt and angry with him/her in the past, but add that you're going to do your best to forgive. Repeat: *"I forgive you and release you. Go your own way and be happy."*

Now write the following: *"I now forgive and release you all."* Then destroy the paper.

Complete the clearing experience by listing the people you feel you have harmed or treated unjustly in the past.

1. _____

2. _____

3. _____

4. _____

5. _____

Reflections

Close your eyes and imagine each person in turn. Tell each of them what you did and ask each to forgive you. Imagine each one doing so unconditionally.

Write the following and repeat it in the space below *"I forgive myself and absolve myself of all guilt, here, now and forever."*

_____

_____

_____

_____

_____

Finally, complete the forgiveness cycle with a positive affirmation.

AFFIRMATION, e.g., *"The more old, negative feelings I release, the more space I create for good things." "I am now putting my life in order, preparing to accept all the good that is coming to me."*

_____

_____

_____

_____

_____

Reflections

How to Set Goals Effectively

Goal-setting is the key that unlocks the door to positive self-esteem. You may want to get together with a group of like-minded friends who are also ready to make changes in their lives. Or you may feel more comfortable working on your own. Just remember, however, that when you hit a snag — and you will — groups are an effective way to get you past the rough spots.

Goal-Setting Traps to Avoid

One of the reasons we don't set goals is that the process itself can cause a certain amount of anxiety. Since goals are dreams with deadlines, they can connect the here and now with the process of achievement.

There are, nevertheless, some traps associated with goal-setting. See if any of these sound familiar.

1. **Overly complex goals.**

   Don't allow yourself to get carried away with goals that are too complex or unattainable.

2. Goals that aren't measurable.

   Maybe you want to be a better parent. How do you know when you've achieved this goal? The never-ending challenge of "being a better parent" will exhaust you, and your guilt won't magically go away.

   Instead, spend some time thinking about what would mean a lot to you and your children. It should involve a measurable amount of time with a definite deadline: say, a camping trip. Get your kids involved in the planning stage so they can share in the excitement.

3. **Goals that aren't what you want, but what you think you should want.**

   Goal-setting is for ourselves, not something we do to please others. Don't get caught up in setting goals that are "sensible" or "mature" or even logical. You may be spending the next year of your life achieving your goal, so make it fun, experimental and meaningful.

4. **Being overly rigid about goals.**

When properly conceived, goals are based on feelings that can be described as "touchstones." A touchstone is a test or criterion for determining whether something is genuine. For instance, your goal may be to become a lawyer, but this goal is actually based on the touchstone of using your intelligence as an advocate for the defenseless. After your first year of law school, you decide that it isn't really what you had hoped. After your second year, you've had enough, and you end up working with the homeless in job training.

Although your goals changed, your touchstone — "helping the defenseless" — did not.

5. **Knowing how to deal with failure when we don't meet goals.**

No one wants to fail. However, there's a lot to be learned from failure. It's like a signpost saying "This goal wasn't appropriate for you. Look over here instead."

Some of the world's greatest success stories are built on failure. Four millionaires, in a recent study, responded that they had set themselves the goal to have $1 million by the age of 35. On an average, each had held 18 jobs before striking it rich. From failure they learned what didn't work for them, and they quickly redirected their energies.

If you have failed to meet a goal, deal with it consciously. Don't push it to the back of your brain. Ask yourself if it is a goal you still wish to pursue or one you want to let go. It's important to acknowledge unattained goals in this way. Otherwise they stack up in the subconscious under the heading of "failures" and create resistance to further goal-setting.

Using Brainstorming to Set Goals

Now you're ready to start setting some goals. Any goal you choose will somehow affect every part of your life. Saving the money to buy a new stereo, for instance, could determine how aggressively you go after a promotion at work. It's important to realize that although our life is compartmentalized into different areas, these are subtly woven together into a single fabric. For example, one type of goal *(a more appropriate career choice)* may be enhanced by meeting another type of goal *(singing lessons for self-expression).*

Think of goals falling into six categories:

1. Work and career.

2. Lifestyle.

3. Relationships.

4. Creative self-expression.

5. Travel and leisure.

6. Personal development/education.

Without thinking too deeply, quickly write down under each of the following categories some goals you would like to achieve. For example, under "Personal development/education" you might list as a goal "earn a bachelor's degree in business."

Work and career:_____

Lifestyle:_____

Relationships: _____

Creative self-expression:_____

Travel and leisure: _____

Personal development/education:_____

Reflections

Prioritizing Your Goals

Once you have completed the "brainstorming" process, your goals need to be ranked in order of importance. When you prioritize which ones you want to work on immediately, you'll see that some are short-term goals (usually less than one year in duration) while some are long-term (longer than three years).

When deciding what's of utmost importance, take the "energy test." If you know someone who's engaged in the same goal-setting process, or have a good friend who is willing to listen (and suspend judgment), have him or her make a tape recording of you describing your goals. Afterwards, when you play the tape, listen to where you put the most energy. You'll hear the tempo of your speaking pattern speed up, grow warm with enthusiasm and glow with confidence when you start talking about the goal that means the most to you.

Using the ideas you developed through brainstorming, convert your brainstorming thoughts to specific, measurable, timebound goals: *I will increase my earnings by 15 percent by January.*

Goal 1: _____

_____

Goal 2: _____

_____

Goal 3: _____

_____

Goal 4: _____

_____

Goal 5: _____

_____

Goal 6: _____

_____

Once you have converted your ideas into specific, measurable, timebound goals, prioritize them in order of importance from 1-6 (1 being the most important/urgent). Which goals do you feel are short-term? Long-term?

Reflections

Short-Term and Long-Term Goals

Goal-setting is most effective when goals can be accomplished within a reasonable period of time. That's where establishing short-term goals can be helpful.

Long-term goals (such as finding meaningful employment) cannot be achieved without setting short-term, achievable monthly or even weekly goals along the way. Think of these as daily stepping stones that eventually lead to that far-off goal on the horizon. Short-term goals need to be updated constantly. It's helpful to have someone to report to on a monthly or even weekly basis.

The feeling of accomplishment gained through short-term goal attainment is highly rewarding. This feeling fuels you to continue pursuing and achieving other short-term milestones on the way to your ultimate long-term goal.

Some long-term goals take three or more years to fully complete. It helps to write down such goals in the form of affirmations, as if they had already been achieved. *"I now do important field research on South American tribes. My work keeps their forests and traditions from disappearing."* Remember when writing one-year goals, for example, that they need to support your three-year goals. They must all flow in the same direction so that when you accomplish your one-year goals, you will be one step closer to reaching your three-year goals.

Next, we need to determine the "hows," or the steps needed to accomplish the goal(s). Be realistic about how much you can accomplish in a month (take the GRE exam) or a week (write application letters to various universities). Accompany these steps with affirmations such as *"I am reaching my goal step-by-step, day-by-day."*

Take two of your long-term goals and determine the steps you will take to reach them. This constitutes your action plan.

GOAL #1: (what you'll achieve)

_____

_____

Plan (how, action steps)	*Date to be accomplished*
1. _____	_____
2. _____	_____
3. _____	_____
4. _____	_____

GOAL #2: (what you'll achieve)

_____

_____

Plan (how, action steps)	*Date to be accomplished*
1. _____	_____
2. _____	_____
3. _____	_____
4. _____	_____

Reflections

The "Motivation" Behind the Goal

Let's say getting a degree is your favorite on the list. That means all your other goals must be of secondary importance. Now, define the "motivation" behind the wish to get a master's in anthropology. Remember, the "motivation" comes behind the goal.

Perhaps you think an M.A. in anthropology will get you a better job. This is information you need to check out. A master's degree in anthropology promises you three years of interesting classes. This translates to "intellectual stimulation with a chance of meaningful employment when completed."

By meeting your primary goal, you also have the chance to fulfill your secondary goals. For example, you could meet stimulating people; you might even travel a bit.

Now take two or three of your goals and evaluate the "motivations" behind them; classify them as short- or long-term goals.

GOAL 1:

_____ Motivation:

___ Long-term or ____Short-term

GOAL 2:

_____ Motivation:

___ Long-term or ____Short-term

GOAL 3:

_____ Motivation:

___ Long-term or ____Short-term

Write an affirmation of a long-term goal. Remember to write as if the goal has already been accomplished!

_____

_____

Reflections

Goal-Attainment Resources

Networking

Working in a support group increases the flow of energy much more than working alone. Have you ever heard famous people talk about how they got where they were going? Great success stories usually contain some particle of starving in garrets, paying one's dues and honing talent through rough times. But eventually, someone loaned the celeb-in-the-making a helping hand and offered him his first lucky break. Working with and through others in this way is called ***networking***.

During this process, you can rely upon others to help out in a number of roles:

As mentors. If you know someone personally who achieved what you wish to achieve or who is successful, ask if you can "interview" that person and have him or her advise you. Believe it or not, most successful people are dying to talk about how they made it and will be happy to share "how-tos." Find out what you can offer in return. All good networking includes reciprocity.

As heroes. Who are your heroes? You may choose heroes for their accomplishments, their bravery, their talents or their kind hearts. Pin up their pictures on a bulletin board or the wall by your desk where they can inspire you daily. Focus on what makes these individuals appropriate role models for you. (Be prepared to be disillusioned. All too often, our heroes turn out to have feet of clay.)

As conduits of information. Perhaps you need to know what kind of crops grew in your area during Neolithic times, or you'd like to look through a telescope just once and have someone explain how it works. You may not have direct access to this kind of information, but almost everyone knows someone who can help you. It may not be quite in the way you envisioned, but networking works. The wider your array of business associates, friends and fellow members in professional groups, the more rewards you reap.

As requesting that you give rather than receive. Groups ensure that your talents are being tapped by helping others. If you have worked in a volunteer capacity, you may have noticed a curious dynamic — eventually, giving to the group becomes more important than what you get out of it.

Summary

Goal-setting boosts self-esteem because, if done correctly, it can get us to where we want to be. Without clear goals, it's too easy to drift through life, never making a commitment to what we truly value. You don't have to know what you want to achieve before you set goals. Often the process of goal-setting will make that clear.

Effective goal-planning

Effective goal-planning takes some practice. Traps to avoid include:

1. Overly complex goals.

2. Non-measurable, undefined goals.

3. Goals that don't reflect your true desires.

4. Being overly rigid about goals once they're defined.

5. Not realizing the benefits of failing to meet a goal — what failure offers is a chance to redefine and re-prioritize.

Preliminary Steps

Some preliminary steps help us set goals more effectively. Clearing, for instance, relies upon getting rid of past patterns, eliminating physical blocks to the flow of energy within your body. Clearing is facilitated by forgiving those who have wronged us and those whom we have wronged. Truly forgiving and releasing old enemies from our consciousness helps get new, creative energies flowing.

Brainstorming

Brainstorming, either alone or with others, is a great way to define goals for various aspects of our lives. Once the goals are objectively listed, we can start prioritizing.

Motivation

Specific goals may change, but the *"motivation"* behind the goal remains the same. Arrange the short-term goals so that they help accomplish the long-term goals.

While long-term goals should reflect our innermost fantasies, our highest ideals or our most exalted visions, we should be able to accomplish them within a specific deadline. After you have stated clearly what you want, networking is one of the most effective ways to achieve your goals by working through others.

After reading this chapter, you will learn:

☑ to physically accept yourself

☑ to have high self-esteem in partnerships

☑ to build self-esteem in your children

4 SELF-ESTEEM AND THE FAMILY

Some say charity begins at home. *So does self-esteem.* In previous chapters we examined the imprinting we received as children and how those messages affected our self-esteem today. Now it's time to look at how we, as adults, nurture self-esteem in other family members — whether partners, children, siblings or aging parents.

The Family as a Movie

We've all seen movies about families, whether they're the creative screwballs in *You Can't Take It with You*, the tragic perfectionists in *Ordinary People* or the heartwarming couple in *It's a Wonderful Life*.

Look at your own family as you would a group of characters in a movie. Think about the roles members in your family have played, beginning with your mother and father and extending to your own children. Does your rebellious daughter remind you of your judgmental mother? Does your husband remind you of your father when he's being particularly aloof? How do those roles change as people age? For example, your parents were probably more lenient with their third child than with their first.

Sometimes roles are assigned to us — even before we are born. We may not like the roles we're given, but we're in the grip of the family. To advocate change means to go against the flow that was established early on in our family's history — who the successful ones would be, who the failures would be — even who is attractive and who is not.

Sometimes the only way to change roles is to change movies — that's why so many people literally blossom once they leave home.

Ask Yourself the Following Questions:

1. Did I trust my parents to value me for the qualities I value in myself?

2. Did my parents encourage autonomy in their children, or did they subconsciously encourage dependence?

3. Did my parents ever discourage me from doing things or from displaying feelings because they were unacceptable for my age or gender?

You may already have explored the nature of your early relationship with your parents or primary caretakers. Adult self-esteem is frequently a reflection of how we internalized our early experiences of trust, reciprocity and autonomy.

Trust. Infants need to know they can count on someone outside themselves to act in a predictable manner.

Reciprocity. The bond between parent and child is strengthened by reciprocal emotions and shared experiences children come to expect and rely on.

Autonomy. Parents need to let the child know they are there without interfering with the child's need to explore and test the outer world.

Adults, like children, progress through these three developmental stages. These act as building blocks toward a healthy personality and high self-esteem.

Reflect on the following questions and record your responses:

1. Do I feel self-conscious when I try to express myself?
   _____ (yes) _____ (no) _____ (sometimes)

   If we learned as children that certain emotions were unacceptable, self-expression may feel threatening.

2. Do I have difficulty confronting people when I think they've acted wrongly toward me or another? _____ (yes) _____ (no) _____ (sometimes)

   If you have trouble confronting people who anger you, ask yourself: Where does my anger usually go? Do I complain to others, or do I act it out in self-destructive patterns?

3. Can I set goals and stick to them? _____ (yes) _____ (no) _____ (sometimes)

   If making a commitment to yourself is a real problem, it may indicate that the sense of commitment was not developed during your childhood.

4. Do I let people take advantage of me? ___ (yes) ___ (no) ___ (sometimes)

   It's healthy to say "no" and have others listen. Perhaps when we said "no" in the past, we didn't sound like we meant it. If you don't enforce your boundaries, no one else will.

5. Do I continue to have similar destructive relationships?

   ___ (yes) ___ (no) ___ (sometimes)

   The way we deal with the world is very similar to the way we dealt with Mom and Dad when we were children. Even if, after vowing intensely to never fall for it again, you still find yourself choosing the same types of partners/friends, maybe it's time to check out your primary caretakers.

Reflections

Breaking the Cycle

Often, as parents we look at ourselves and our accomplishments and wish for the opportunity to "replay the tape" or relive our lives. Thoughts such as "If only I'd chosen a different career…," "Why did I marry so young?" or "Why didn't I pay more attention to the way I looked before it was too late?" are constant reminders of the physical, professional and personal "shortcomings" we all experience. Sometimes, we find ourselves wanting the best for our children so badly that we project our own feelings of inadequacy onto our children through overly critical comments and unrealistic goals.

To break this cycle of inadequacy, we must learn to accept ourselves — both our positive and negative characteristics — in a healthy, self-affirming way. This is not to say that we should simply "give up" our quest for continual self-development and improvement. It means that we must first accept ourselves before we can accept those closest to us — our spouse, friends, coworkers and children.

"Physical" Self Acceptance

How you feel physically plays a big part in self-esteem and self-acceptance. Just because a person is in shape doesn't mean he doesn't suffer from self-doubt, fear or depression like so many others.

Women, especially, link body image to self-esteem. In the beginning of her career, Jane Fonda resorted to starvation through obsessive dieting and laxative abuse that led to bulimia and anorexia. It wasn't until Fonda discovered alternatives through proper eating habits and regular exercise that she overcame these destructive habits.

Oddly enough, a "thinner you" doesn't always mean a "happier you." A recent study of 682 coeds in a Midwest university revealed a clear relationship between eating disorders, unhealthy behavior to control weight and diminished self-esteem.

Although the study was evenly divided between men and women averaging 19 years of age, the body-image/self-esteem relationship was considerably greater among the women. Even when the subjects fell within a normal weight range, the women tended to consider themselves 10 pounds overweight, while the men tended to consider themselves only three pounds overweight.

Becoming obsessed about your weight is detrimental to your psychological health because you:

- Emphasize how you look over how you feel.

- Are kept in a vicious cycle of weight loss followed by unavoidable weight gain once you are off the diet.

- Damage your self-esteem.

For the next exercise you need a hand-held mirror. Take a deep breath and close your eyes. Think of how you look in the full-length mirror when you're dressing in the morning — imperfections and all. Concentrate on the present, how you look and feel. Keep your breathing regular and relaxed. Imagine that your image in the mirror emanates from your innermost being — it's filled with love and healing energy. See it pulsating all around you. It feels warm and caressing. Now slowly open your eyes and look in the mirror. Repeat these word: *"I love and accept you exactly as you are."*

When some people do this exercise, they feel calm and happy. Others start criticizing the person they see in the mirror. Suspend all critical thoughts. It's okay if you feel frightened or sad. Just look into your eyes in the mirror and repeat: *"I love and accept you exactly as you are."* What do you feel now?

Do this exercise daily for the next 21 days and record your progress on the next page.

Reflections

Day/Date	Reaction	Trends I see developing	Was there any external event that affected my reaction? (Y/N)
Day 1 _____			
Day 2 _____			
Day 3 _____			
Day 4 _____			
Day 5 _____			
Day 6 _____			
Day 7 _____			
Day 8 _____			
Day 9 _____			
Day 10 _____			
Day 11 _____			
Day 12 _____			
Day 13 _____			
Day 14 _____			
Day 15 _____			
Day 16 _____			
Day 17 _____			
Day 18 _____			
Day 19 _____			
Day 20 _____			
Day 21 _____			

Reflections

Self-Esteem in Partnerships

Statistics show that women whose husbands physically abuse them were often abused by their fathers. As a species, humans seem to like patterns, good or bad. Low self-esteem dictates that we seek demeaning situations and stay there — no matter how much we have to manipulate others or lie to ourselves to be able to do so.

On the other hand, healthy relationships based on high self-esteem allow partners to experience a great deal of personal freedom while expressing their love for one another. Roles aren't assigned based on traditions, sexual stereotypes or neurotic patterning, but on perceived needs and ways to meet them. Perhaps you really like to sculpt in metal whereas your spouse or partner likes to cook. There are no rules, except to do what you really enjoy.

Respect is another earmark of a solid relationship. People with high self-esteem have a healthy respect for themselves. Two people who respect themselves and each other are like a pair of powerful horses who can pull each other through life's quagmires and cross the finish line a winning team.

Traditionally, relationships have exacted a higher price on women's self-esteem than men's. Recent studies show both men and women bear the burden of caring for aging parents — up to 18 years. Add child-care responsibilities and the great likelihood of blending split family agendas and there's not much time for self-expression.

Obviously, most of the old role expectations still linger. Some relationships are based entirely on rules — about what's appropriate for men and what's appropriate for women; about what I get to do if you get to do this. Eventually, the price for self-expression becomes so high that partners simply stop paying it.

Take a minute and reflect on how traditional expectations may still be impacting your life.

Yes No Sometimes

❏   ❏   ❏   1. Are you tempted to solve everyone else's problems at the expense of your own needs?

You've asked your mate to do the dishes every other night, but he begins to sulk. Do you give in to his emotional pressure and wash the dishes or do you say, "You've got a problem. Deal with it."

❏   ❏   ❏   2. Do you routinely try to "fix" the problem?

When you complain, how does your mate react? See if fixing his/her problem is based upon your fear of losing the relationship you are dependent upon.

❏   ❏   ❏   3. Do you feel it's a woman's place to "make everyone happy"?

You want to take an evening class, and you need the family car. When your mate responds negatively, do you continue the class or do you drop it?

❏   ❏   ❏   4. Can you strike the balance between feeling empathy for others' feelings and self-interest?

It is possible to acknowledge another person's feelings without becoming a compulsive caretaker. To do so, you need to figure out your priorities.

Begin to move to the "no" response for questions 1, 2 and 3 and "yes" for question 4. Such a change will assist you in improving the partnership's self-esteem and respect.

Reflections

Building Self-Esteem in Your Children

You think you're doing pretty well with your kids. Then one day, you're pushed to the brink. After a bad day at work, you ask your 10-year-old to clean up his room, but two hours later, nothing's been done. *"What's the matter with you?"* you scream. *"Don't you ever listen to what I say? You're lazy and selfish."*

With an overwhelming sense of guilt, you realize you just replayed one of your old tapes from your own childhood. You try to make amends and apologize. Your son mumbles that it's okay, but you know it's not.

The relationship we have with our children is probably the most important one in our lives because we're responsible for shaping a human being's social reactions from the moment of birth.

Our children's world can be very scary if they don't feel good about themselves. Since they have few experiences to compare their reality against, home becomes their universe. If their parents are overly critical, blaming, judgmental or quick to punish, children have little recourse but to internalize the concept that they are "bad."

Children are almost conditioned to internalize guilt. When their parents are divorcing, for instance, children usually feel it is their fault. Even children of physically abusive parents feel they are somehow to blame.

Therefore, *one of the greatest gifts you can give your child is the gift of self-esteem.* Think of esteem building as setting a pattern your children will pass on to their children, and on through the generations. In equipping your children with self-respect and self-acceptance, you might even break the pattern of centuries of negative conditioning.

Here's How to Start:

Accept, don't deny, feelings. Since parents can often act as the guardians of their children's feelings, you need to be sensitive about how you react.

Sometimes we deny feelings to get children to stop behaving in a way we find annoying. For example, on your way home after taking your son to the dentist, he's complaining about how much his tooth hurts from the filling. Rather than acknowledging his feelings, you say irritably *"Come on. Stop whining. It can't hurt that much."*

When children's feelings are brushed aside in this manner, they may become angry.

Identify a situation with a child that requires you to accept his or her feeling.

_____

_____

_____

_____

Make sure you:

- Listen actively, giving the child your full attention.

- Resist the temptation to jump in and "fix" the complaint. Instead, reflect the child's feelings through questions or statements that indicate you heard what he said.

- Experience the empowerment that comes with being genuinely helpful.

What kind of results did you achieve? How were they different from other situations you've experienced?

_____

_____

_____

_____

_____

_____

_____

Reflections

Controlling Your Emotions

It might feel strange at first not to shift the emotional burden from your child, but you'll be surprised how eagerly she'll open up and continue giving you information. Eventually, through the dialogue, you'll come to a resolution.

Avoid blaming, accusing, name-calling and use of threats. Nothing is more damaging to a child's fragile self-esteem than to be called *"stupid"* or *"a slob,"* or to be told that the way he eats is *"disgusting."*

The goal is to engage cooperation. You can't do everything it takes to run a house, help with homework, get yourself ready for work and tend to your kids' daily crises all alone. Besides, you want your children to assume responsibility and learn how to participate, be more able to share.

For instance, your 8-year-old daughter begged to get a dog. You explained that the family could have a dog, as long as she would feed it and take it for a walk once a day. You come home from work and find that the dog hasn't been out of the backyard and is completely out of water. You explode at your daughter, saying, *"You don't deserve to have a pet! I told you what the conditions were."*

Take time out, breathe deeply, and try this new approach:

- **Describe the situation.** Look out the window and say, *"I see Brandy pacing up and down in front of the gate."* Try to avoid adding manipulative phrases like, *"Sure looks like he wants to take a walk."*

- **Give information.** Instead of nagging, *"How many times have I told you to be sure that Brandy has water on hot days?"* say, *"The dog's water dish is empty."*

- **Talk about your feelings.** If your daughter's whining about having to take the dog for a walk is getting on your nerves, tell her, *"Honey, I need to concentrate on getting dinner organized right now. I don't appreciate the whining. Maybe you'd like to switch jobs. You can fix the green beans and I'll take the dog out."*

When your children fail to cooperate on a simple household task, don't lecture or berate them. Rather, tell them why it's important to you that they do what they're supposed to do. *"I don't like Brandy being neglected when we agreed the dog is your responsibility. Remember, we decided on this before we got Brandy."*

Be willing to listen to the child's agenda, too. Maybe taking care of the dog on a daily basis is too much responsibility for your daughter. Take time to listen to her feelings. Maybe there's an underlying message. She's frightened that she'll lose control of the dog while he's on the leash. Keep the discussion open. Let her know your feelings, too. Enlist your children's help in reprioritizing and problem-solving.

• **Show the big picture.** *"If we take Brandy for a walk now, that means dinner will be an hour late. Can you wait that long?"* It helps for children to know about cause and effect.

When children cause problems by misbehaving, discipline can be either harsh, lenient or somewhere in between. Parents who are strict disciplinarians often bend their child's will to coincide with their own, allowing them little say in how problems are resolved. Complete leniency, on the other hand, is no solution either. By misbehaving, children often push for guidelines. They want to know where the limits are.

• **Talk about your child's feelings and needs.** You can open the discussion by saying, *"I know it probably isn't easy for you to leave your friends when you're playing Nintendo."* This lets him know you're not presenting the situation from your viewpoint alone. It invites him to comment, to explain, to expand.

• **Talk about your feelings.** *"But you know, I worry when you're late. I worry when I can't find you."* Let him see the situation through your eyes and understand your true concern.

• **Brainstorm a solution.** Ask for input. Say, *"Let's put our heads together and see if we can come up with some ideas that would be good for both of us."* As the child makes suggestions, write them down. When you're through brainstorming, take a look at your list and see what solutions you want to keep.

- **Reward kids for doing it right.** When your child actually does what you've asked her to, be sure to reward her positively. Do not act like good behavior is simply expected. The reward can be as simple as a hug or the smile in your voice she hears over the phone.

  Conversely, children need to understand that failing to fulfill the terms of an agreement has its consequences. Whether you discipline your child by taking away his freedom or having a serious discussion, he needs to know the laws of cause and effect and that he can choose between right and wrong behavior. Punishment should always be accompanied by an explanation of why you're taking such action.

- **Give children a sense of autonomy.** Children need to know they can function successfully outside the home. As they grow older, give them more responsibilities and allow them more freedom to move out into the world and explore. Give them information about how to take care of themselves, but teach them the world can be a safe place.

By encouraging your young teenage daughter to take on baby-sitting jobs, you accomplish several goals: She develops a source of income and with it the decision to save or spend money; she has meaningful interaction with younger children for whom she might act as a role model; she sees how other families live. It's important for children to learn how other families are different from and similar to their own.

Encourage children to be productive members of groups: Boy Scouts or Girl Scouts, basketball teams, the school play. Don't rush in to correct the mistakes you think your child is making. Allow your child to live with the consequences of his or her choices. Self-esteem doesn't come from always having done the "right thing."

Realize that your child has his own unique path to follow. As he grows up and becomes more autonomous, your role as adviser, helper and mentor needs to lessen in significance. After holding on tightly, letting go lightly can be difficult.

Apply the visualization skills you learned to improve your family's self-esteem by letting go or releasing negative thoughts and emotions.

Close your eyes and breathe deeply. See yourself as a child, maybe five or six, just playing around the house and then in the yard with friends. See your parents when you were this age. Experience the feelings you had then. *Did you feel loved and accepted by your parents or did they often fly off the handle, blaming and accusing you for everything that went wrong?* Touch briefly on that center of pain within you that may be caused by blaming yourself at such a vulnerable age.

Record your feelings as a *child*.

_____

_____

_____

Now realize that you are an adult. You can forgive your parents for the pain they may have caused you. Repeat whichever affirmations seem right: *"I have all the love I need within my own heart." "I am letting go of the old and making way for the new."* By forgiving your parents and releasing negative thoughts and emotions, you allow yourself to be a source of healing for your own children.

Write an affirmation that forgives your parents and repeat it aloud:

_____

_____

_____

Reflections

Finally, picture your child as clearly as you can. Ask him if there is anything he would like for you to do for him. You may hear the words *"I need your love, Daddy,"* or *"I want you to spend more time with me."* See all your child's problems dissolve.

Record what you heard your child say and work on meeting the need or request expressed:

_____

_____

_____

_____

_____

_____

_____

_____

_____

_____

You might want to say an affirmation created especially for this child about how much you love him, value him and always will be there for him.

Reflections

Summary

People are assigned roles in families just like roles are assigned in movies. If you feel "typecast" in a role you've outgrown or are no longer comfortable with, changing it is not always easy.

Building self-esteem is a major step toward circumventing your family's negative definitions and false expectations so you don't unconsciously continue to play the role you were handed. One way of building your self-esteem within the family is to realize there are no "good" or "bad" ways of being, there are simply preferences.

Another esteem-building tactic is to research your family's history. Get family members to talk about their past: their childhood on the farm, their young adulthood surviving the Depression. It's a good way to discard institutionalized family roles and get a glimpse of your parents the way they were.

Building self-esteem in your children is an investment in the future. In some cases, you'll be breaking a chain of inherited abuse — whether resentment, criticism, bullying or faultfinding. You can build your child's self-esteem by following a few simple steps:

1. Accept, don't deny, his feelings.

2. When disciplining your child, avoid blaming, accusing, name-calling and threats. The goal is to engage cooperation, set limits and teach your child self-discipline, not to breed resentment and rebellion. You can do this by describing the situation that needs attention; giving your child information about cause and effect; discussing your feelings honestly; showing the big picture of a process.

3. Invite children to be problem solvers, not problem causers, by talking about their feelings and needs and your feelings and then together brainstorming a solution.

4. A child's self-esteem grows in proportion to the amount of autonomy she experiences — first within, and then beyond the family. To prepare your child to function successfully in the outside world, give her plenty of "how-tos"; encourage her to get an appropriate job and exercise control over her own money; support her as she makes her own decisions (right or wrong).

5 INVESTING IN YOUR SELF-ESTEEM

Building a stronger self-esteem is one of the most important things you can ever do for yourself. You can change your life by changing how you feel about life. When you're coming from a better place, the bad times are less threatening, and the good times are more frequent.

It's a common fallacy to believe that our lives will improve once a certain event occurs or once we acquire a long-coveted possession. If we examine our desires closely, it's easy to see that attaining them will not bring true happiness, only momentary fulfillment. Both happiness and change must come from within.

Self-esteem begins when we honestly examine our emotions. For example, how we feel towards others tells us a great deal about how we, as children, felt toward ourselves. Negative habits such as judging and criticizing others, for instance, can be overcome when we cease to judge and criticize others.

Two important tools in this process are affirmations and visualization. By repeatedly focusing on the positive and giving your subconscious a new verbal and visual "blueprint" for the future, you'll soon see results in an improved self-image. No matter what kind of childhood you had, building your self-esteem will put you in touch with your own inner power.

Think of building your self-esteem as an investment in the future. Psychologically healthy adults have healthier children who are less prone to self-destructive behavior.

So what have you got to lose? Make that investment in yourself. It's one investment you'll never regret.

Ten Attitudes of Self-Esteem

The ten attitude basics that can help are as follows:

1. **Be your own best friend.** Encourage and love yourself. Don't expect yourself to be perfect. Give yourself a break!

2. **Take time to enjoy your life.** Choose something that you enjoy and schedule it into your life, just as you would schedule an important doctor's appointment. Make it a priority.

3. **Let go of the past.** Let go of the hurt, the anger, the disillusionments and the guilt. If they creep back into your life, let go of them again and again.

4. **Set goals for your life.** On a regular basis, review your short- and long-term goals. Don't be afraid to reach high.

5. **Talk positively to yourself.** Use affirmations to give your subconscious a powerful positive message. Harness the energy that lies within you to move you towards your chosen goal.

6. **Visualize your success behavior.** In every aspect of your life, visualize yourself achieving your goal. Experience the emotions and enjoyment of accomplishing what you have set out to do. Become what you think.

7. **Make choices for your life.** You are free to change, free to grow, free to choose how you will live the rest of your life.

8. **Network with others.** Learn to rely on others for information, support and role behaviors. You don't have to do it alone.

9. **Write your own family script.** Decide the role that you wish to play in your family movie. Follow the script that you have written, rather than the script that has been written for you by the expectations and decisions of others.

10. **Accept yourself as you are.** Love yourself — physically, mentally, and emotionally — as you would love a dear friend. Gently encourage this friend to grow, not by criticizing, but by loving acceptance.

Index

Notes

Notes

Notes

Buy any 3, get 1 FREE!

Get a 60-Minute Training Series™ Handbook FREE ($14.95 value)*
when you buy any three. See back of order form for full selection of titles.

These are helpful how-to books for you, your employees and co-workers. Add to your library. Use for new-employee training, brown-bag seminars, promotion gifts and more. Choose from many popular titles on a variety of lifestyle, communication, productivity and leadership topics. Exclusively from National Press Publications.

BUY 3 GET 1 FREE!
Buy more, save more!

DESKTOP HANDBOOK ORDER FORM

Ordering is easy:

1. Complete both sides of this Order Form, detach, and mail, fax or phone your order to:

> **Mail:** National Press Publications
> P.O. Box 419107
> Kansas City, MO 64141-6107

> **Fax:** 1-913-432-0824
> **Phone:** 1-800-258-7248
> **Internet:** www.natsem.com

2. Please print:

Name_____ Position/Title _____

Company/Organization_____

Address_____City _____

State/Province_____ZIP/Postal Code _____

Telephone (____)_____ Fax (____) _____

Your e-mail: _____

3. Easy payment:

❏ Enclosed is my check or money order for $_____ (total from back).
Please make payable to National Press Publications.

Please charge to:
❏ MasterCard ❏ VISA ❏ American Express

Credit Card No. _____ Exp. Date_____

Signature_____

● ●
MORE WAYS TO SAVE:

SAVE 33%!!! BUY 20-50 COPIES of any title ... pay just $9.95 each ($11.25 Canadian).

SAVE 40%!!! BUY 51 COPIES OR MORE of any title ... pay just $8.95 each ($10.25 Canadian).

* $20.00 in Canada

Buy 3, get 1 FREE!
60-MINUTE TRAINING SERIES™ HANDBOOKS

TITLE	RETAIL PRICE	QTY	TOTAL
8 Steps for Highly Effective Negotiations #424	$14.95		
Assertiveness #4422	$14.95		
Balancing Career and Family #4152	$14.95		
Common Ground #4122	$14.95		
Delegate for Results #4592	$14.95		
The Essentials of Business Writing #4310	$14.95		
Everyday Parenting Solutions #4862	$14.95		
Exceptional Customer Service #4882	$14.95		
Fear & Anger: Slay the Dragons … #4302	$14.95		
Fundamentals of Planning #4301	$14.95		
Getting Things Done #4112	$14.95		
How to Coach an Effective Team #4308	$14.95		
How to De-Junk Your Life #4306	$14.95		
How to Handle Conflict and Confrontation #4952	$14.95		
How to Manage Your Boss #493	$14.95		
How to Supervise People #4102	$14.95		
How to Work With People #4032	$14.95		
Inspire & Motivate: Performance Reviews #4232	$14.95		
Listen Up: Hear What's Really Being Said #4172	$14.95		
Motivation and Goal-Setting #4962	$14.95		
A New Attitude #4432	$14.95		
The New Dynamic Comm. Skills for Women #4309	$14.95		
The Polished Professional #4262	$14.95		
The Power of Innovative Thinking #428	$14.95		
The Power of Self-Managed Teams #4222	$14.95		
Powerful Communication Skills #4132	$14.95		
Present With Confidence #4612	$14.95		
The Secret to Developing Peak Performers #4692	$14.95		
Self-Esteem: The Power to Be Your Best #4642	$14.95		
Shortcuts to Organized Files & Records #4307	$14.95		
The Stress Management Handbook #4842	$14.95		
Supreme Teams: How to Make Teams Work #4303	$14.95		
Thriving on Change #4212	$14.95		
Women and Leadership #4632	$14.95		

Sales Tax
All purchases subject to
state and local sales tax.
Questions?
Call
1-800-258-7248

Subtotal	$
Add 7% Sales Tax (*Or add appropriate state and local tax*)	$
Shipping and Handling (*$3 one item; 50¢ each additional item*)	$
TOTAL	$

08/01